OH, THE PLACES I HAVE GONE!

TRAVEL JOURNAL FOR TEENS

INSPIRA
JOURNALS, PLANNERS &
NOTEBOOKS

THIS JOURNAL BELONGS TO:

TRAVEL JOURNAL

When: ....

Days: ....

Where: ....

Location ....

To do before leaving:

✓ ....
✓ ....

✓ ....
✓ ....

✓ ....
✓ ....

✓ ....
✓ ....

✓ ....
✓ ....

✓ ....
✓ ....

✓ ....
✓ ....

Packing Checklist:

✓ ....
✓ ....

✓ ....
✓ ....

✓ ....
✓ ....

✓ ....
✓ ....

✓ ....
✓ ....

✓ ....
✓ ....

✓ ....
✓ ....

✓ ....
✓ ....

WRITE THE DETAILS OR DRAW THEM HERE.

HOW WAS YOUR TRAVEL?

- ◯ Fun
- ◯ Amazing
- ◯ Fine
- ◯ Crazy
- ◯ Exciting
- ◯ Boring
- ◯ Exhausting

YOUR MOOD

YOUR RATING

RATE IT!

TRAVEL JOURNAL

When: ....

Days: ....

Where: ....

Location ....

To do before leaving:

- ✓ ....
- ✓ ....
- ✓ ....
- ✓ ....
- ✓ ....
- ✓ ....
- ✓ ....

- ✓ ....
- ✓ ....
- ✓ ....
- ✓ ....
- ✓ ....
- ✓ ....
- ✓ ....

Packing Checklist:

- ✓ ....
- ✓ ....
- ✓ ....
- ✓ ....
- ✓ ....
- ✓ ....
- ✓ ....

- ✓ ....
- ✓ ....
- ✓ ....
- ✓ ....
- ✓ ....
- ✓ ....
- ✓ ....

WRITE THE DETAILS OR DRAW THEM HERE.

HOW WAS YOUR TRAVEL?

- ○ Fun
- ○ Amazing
- ○ Fine
- ○ Crazy
- ○ Exciting
- ○ Boring
- ○ Exhausting

YOUR MOOD

YOUR RATING

RATE IT!

NOTES (Observations, stories and encounters)

TRAVEL JOURNAL

When: ....   Days: ....

Where: ....

Location ....

To do before leaving:

- ✓ ....
- ✓ ....
- ✓ ....
- ✓ ....
- ✓ ....
- ✓ ....
- ✓ ....

- ✓ ....
- ✓ ....
- ✓ ....
- ✓ ....
- ✓ ....
- ✓ ....
- ✓ ....

Packing Checklist:

- ✓ ....
- ✓ ....
- ✓ ....
- ✓ ....
- ✓ ....
- ✓ ....
- ✓ ....
- ✓ ....

- ✓ ....
- ✓ ....
- ✓ ....
- ✓ ....
- ✓ ....
- ✓ ....
- ✓ ....
- ✓ ....

WRITE THE DETAILS OR DRAW THEM HERE.

HOW WAS YOUR TRAVEL?

- ◯ Fun
- ◯ Amazing
- ◯ Fine
- ◯ Crazy
- ◯ Exciting
- ◯ Boring
- ◯ Exhausting

YOUR MOOD

YOUR RATING

RATE IT!

TRAVEL JOURNAL

When: ....   Days: ....

Where: ....

Location ....

To do before leaving:

✓ ....   ✓ ....

✓ ....   ✓ ....

✓ ....   ✓ ....

✓ ....   ✓ ....

✓ ....   ✓ ....

✓ ....   ✓ ....

✓ ....   ✓ ....

Packing Checklist:

✓ ....   ✓ ....

✓ ....   ✓ ....

✓ ....   ✓ ....

✓ ....   ✓ ....

✓ ....   ✓ ....

✓ ....   ✓ ....

✓ ....   ✓ ....

✓ ....   ✓ ....

WRITE THE DETAILS OR DRAW THEM HERE.

HOW WAS YOUR TRAVEL?

- ◯ Fun
- ◯ Amazing
- ◯ Fine
- ◯ Crazy
- ◯ Exciting
- ◯ Boring
- ◯ Exhausting

YOUR MOOD

YOUR RATING

RATE IT!

TRAVEL JOURNAL

When: ....   Days: ....

Where: ....

Location ....

To do before leaving:

✓ ....   ✓ ....

✓ ....   ✓ ....

✓ ....   ✓ ....

✓ ....   ✓ ....

✓ ....   ✓ ....

✓ ....   ✓ ....

✓ ....   ✓ ....

Packing Checklist:

✓ ....   ✓ ....

✓ ....   ✓ ....

✓ ....   ✓ ....

✓ ....   ✓ ....

✓ ....   ✓ ....

✓ ....   ✓ ....

✓ ....   ✓ ....

✓ ....   ✓ ....

WRITE THE DETAILS OR DRAW THEM HERE.

HOW WAS YOUR TRAVEL?

- ◯ Fun
- ◯ Amazing
- ◯ Fine
- ◯ Crazy
- ◯ Exciting
- ◯ Boring
- ◯ Exhausting

YOUR MOOD

YOUR RATING

RATE IT!

TRAVEL JOURNAL

When: ....   Days: ....

Where: ....

Location ....

To do before leaving:

- [ ] ....   [ ] ....
- [ ] ....   [ ] ....
- [ ] ....   [ ] ....
- [ ] ....   [ ] ....
- [ ] ....   [ ] ....
- [ ] ....   [ ] ....
- [ ] ....   [ ] ....

Packing Checklist:

- [ ] ....   [ ] ....
- [ ] ....   [ ] ....
- [ ] ....   [ ] ....
- [ ] ....   [ ] ....
- [ ] ....   [ ] ....
- [ ] ....   [ ] ....
- [ ] ....   [ ] ....
- [ ] ....   [ ] ....

WRITE THE DETAILS OR DRAW THEM HERE.

HOW WAS YOUR TRAVEL?

○ Fun

○ Amazing

○ Fine

○ Crazy

○ Exciting

○ Boring

○ Exhausting

YOUR MOOD

YOUR RATING

RATE IT!

TRAVEL JOURNAL

When: ....

Days: ....

Where: ....

Location ....

To do before leaving:

- ✓ ....
- ✓ ....
- ✓ ....
- ✓ ....
- ✓ ....
- ✓ ....
- ✓ ....

- ✓ ....
- ✓ ....
- ✓ ....
- ✓ ....
- ✓ ....
- ✓ ....
- ✓ ....

Packing Checklist:

- ✓ ....
- ✓ ....
- ✓ ....
- ✓ ....
- ✓ ....
- ✓ ....
- ✓ ....

- ✓ ....
- ✓ ....
- ✓ ....
- ✓ ....
- ✓ ....
- ✓ ....
- ✓ ....

WRITE THE DETAILS OR DRAW THEM HERE.

HOW WAS YOUR TRAVEL?

- ⃝ Fun
- ⃝ Amazing
- ⃝ Fine
- ⃝ Crazy
- ⃝ Exciting
- ⃝ Boring
- ⃝ Exhausting

YOUR MOOD

YOUR RATING

RATE IT!

TRAVEL JOURNAL

When: ....   Days: ....

Where: ....

Location ....

To do before leaving:

✓ ....   ✓ ....

✓ ....   ✓ ....

✓ ....   ✓ ....

✓ ....   ✓ ....

✓ ....   ✓ ....

✓ ....   ✓ ....

✓ ....   ✓ ....

Packing Checklist:

✓ ....   ✓ ....

✓ ....   ✓ ....

✓ ....   ✓ ....

✓ ....   ✓ ....

✓ ....   ✓ ....

✓ ....   ✓ ....

✓ ....   ✓ ....

✓ ....   ✓ ....

WRITE THE DETAILS OR DRAW THEM HERE.

HOW WAS YOUR TRAVEL?

- ○ Fun
- ○ Amazing
- ○ Fine
- ○ Crazy
- ○ Exciting
- ○ Boring
- ○ Exhausting

YOUR MOOD

YOUR RATING

RATE IT!

TRAVEL JOURNAL

When: ....   Days: ....

Where: ....

Location ....

To do before leaving:

✓ ....   ✓ ....

✓ ....   ✓ ....

✓ ....   ✓ ....

✓ ....   ✓ ....

✓ ....   ✓ ....

✓ ....   ✓ ....

✓ ....   ✓ ....

Packing Checklist:

✓ ....   ✓ ....

✓ ....   ✓ ....

✓ ....   ✓ ....

✓ ....   ✓ ....

✓ ....   ✓ ....

✓ ....   ✓ ....

✓ ....   ✓ ....

✓ ....   ✓ ....

WRITE THE DETAILS OR DRAW THEM HERE.

HOW WAS YOUR TRAVEL?

○ Fun

○ Amazing

○ Fine

○ Crazy

○ Exciting

○ Boring

○ Exhausting

YOUR MOOD

YOUR RATING

RATE IT!

NOTES (Observations, stories and encounters)

TRAVEL JOURNAL

When: ....

Days: ....

Where: ....

Location ....

To do before leaving:

- [x] ....
- [x] ....
- [x] ....
- [x] ....
- [x] ....
- [x] ....
- [x] ....

- [x] ....
- [x] ....
- [x] ....
- [x] ....
- [x] ....
- [x] ....
- [x] ....

Packing Checklist:

- [x] ....
- [x] ....
- [x] ....
- [x] ....
- [x] ....
- [x] ....
- [x] ....

- [x] ....
- [x] ....
- [x] ....
- [x] ....
- [x] ....
- [x] ....
- [x] ....

WRITE THE DETAILS OR DRAW THEM HERE.

HOW WAS YOUR TRAVEL?

- ◯ Fun
- ◯ Amazing
- ◯ Fine
- ◯ Crazy
- ◯ Exciting
- ◯ Boring
- ◯ Exhausting

YOUR MOOD

YOUR RATING

RATE IT!

TRAVEL JOURNAL

When: .... Days: ....

Where: ....

Location ....

To do before leaving:

✓ .... ✓ ....

✓ .... ✓ ....

✓ .... ✓ ....

✓ .... ✓ ....

✓ .... ✓ ....

✓ .... ✓ ....

✓ .... ✓ ....

Packing Checklist:

✓ .... ✓ ....

✓ .... ✓ ....

✓ .... ✓ ....

✓ .... ✓ ....

✓ .... ✓ ....

✓ .... ✓ ....

✓ .... ✓ ....

WRITE THE DETAILS OR DRAW THEM HERE.

HOW WAS YOUR TRAVEL?

- ◯ Fun
- ◯ Amazing
- ◯ Fine
- ◯ Crazy
- ◯ Exciting
- ◯ Boring
- ◯ Exhausting

YOUR MOOD

YOUR RATING

RATE IT!

NOTES (Observations, stories and encounters)

Travel makes one modest, you see what
a tiny place you occupy in the world.
—Gustave Flaubert

One's destination is never a place, but always a new way of seeing things.
—Henry Miller

TRAVEL JOURNAL

When: ....   Days: ....

Where: ....

Location ....

To do before leaving:

✓ ....   ✓ ....

✓ ....   ✓ ....

✓ ....   ✓ ....

✓ ....   ✓ ....

✓ ....   ✓ ....

✓ ....   ✓ ....

✓ ....   ✓ ....

Packing Checklist:

✓ ....   ✓ ....

✓ ....   ✓ ....

✓ ....   ✓ ....

✓ ....   ✓ ....

✓ ....   ✓ ....

✓ ....   ✓ ....

✓ ....   ✓ ....

✓ ....   ✓ ....

WRITE THE DETAILS OR DRAW THEM HERE.

HOW WAS YOUR TRAVEL?

○ Fun

○ Amazing

○ Fine

○ Crazy

○ Exciting

○ Boring

○ Exhausting

YOUR MOOD

YOUR RATING

RATE IT!

TRAVEL JOURNAL

When: ....   Days: ....

Where: ....

Location ....

To do before leaving:

✓ ....   ✓ ....

✓ ....   ✓ ....

✓ ....   ✓ ....

✓ ....   ✓ ....

✓ ....   ✓ ....

✓ ....   ✓ ....

✓ ....   ✓ ....

Packing Checklist:

✓ ....   ✓ ....

✓ ....   ✓ ....

✓ ....   ✓ ....

✓ ....   ✓ ....

✓ ....   ✓ ....

✓ ....   ✓ ....

✓ ....   ✓ ....

✓ ....   ✓ ....

WRITE THE DETAILS OR DRAW THEM HERE.

HOW WAS YOUR TRAVEL?

- ◯ Fun
- ◯ Amazing
- ◯ Fine
- ◯ Crazy
- ◯ Exciting
- ◯ Boring
- ◯ Exhausting

YOUR MOOD

YOUR RATING

RATE IT!

TRAVEL JOURNAL

When: .... Days: ....

Where: ....

Location ....

To do before leaving:

✓ .... ✓ ....

✓ .... ✓ ....

✓ .... ✓ ....

✓ .... ✓ ....

✓ .... ✓ ....

✓ .... ✓ ....

✓ .... ✓ ....

Packing Checklist:

✓ .... ✓ ....

✓ .... ✓ ....

✓ .... ✓ ....

✓ .... ✓ ....

✓ .... ✓ ....

✓ .... ✓ ....

✓ .... ✓ ....

✓ .... ✓ ....

WRITE THE DETAILS OR DRAW THEM HERE.

HOW WAS YOUR TRAVEL?

- ○ Fun
- ○ Amazing
- ○ Fine
- ○ Crazy
- ○ Exciting
- ○ Boring
- ○ Exhausting

YOUR MOOD

YOUR RATING

RATE IT!

NOTES (Observations, stories and encounters)

TRAVEL JOURNAL

When: ....   Days: ....

Where: ....

Location ....

To do before leaving:

✓ ....   ✓ ....

✓ ....   ✓ ....

✓ ....   ✓ ....

✓ ....   ✓ ....

✓ ....   ✓ ....

✓ ....   ✓ ....

✓ ....   ✓ ....

Packing Checklist:

✓ ....   ✓ ....

✓ ....   ✓ ....

✓ ....   ✓ ....

✓ ....   ✓ ....

✓ ....   ✓ ....

✓ ....   ✓ ....

✓ ....   ✓ ....

✓ ....   ✓ ....

WRITE THE DETAILS OR DRAW THEM HERE.

HOW WAS YOUR TRAVEL?

○ Fun

○ Amazing

○ Fine

○ Crazy

○ Exciting

○ Boring

○ Exhausting

YOUR MOOD

YOUR RATING

RATE IT!

TRAVEL JOURNAL

When: ....   Days: ....

Where: ....

Location ....

To do before leaving:

☑ ....   ☑ ....

☑ ....   ☑ ....

☑ ....   ☑ ....

☑ ....   ☑ ....

☑ ....   ☑ ....

☑ ....   ☑ ....

☑ ....   ☑ ....

Packing Checklist:

☑ ....   ☑ ....

☑ ....   ☑ ....

☑ ....   ☑ ....

☑ ....   ☑ ....

☑ ....   ☑ ....

☑ ....   ☑ ....

☑ ....   ☑ ....

☑ ....   ☑ ....

WRITE THE DETAILS OR DRAW THEM HERE.

HOW WAS YOUR TRAVEL?

- ◯ Fun
- ◯ Amazing
- ◯ Fine
- ◯ Crazy
- ◯ Exciting
- ◯ Boring
- ◯ Exhausting

YOUR MOOD

YOUR RATING

RATE IT!

☆ ☆ ☆ ☆ ☆ ☆ ☆ ☆ ☆ ☆

NOTES (Observations, stories and encounters)

TRAVEL JOURNAL

When: .... Days: ....

Where: ....

Location ....

To do before leaving:

✓ .... ✓ ....

✓ .... ✓ ....

✓ .... ✓ ....

✓ .... ✓ ....

✓ .... ✓ ....

✓ .... ✓ ....

✓ .... ✓ ....

Packing Checklist:

✓ .... ✓ ....

✓ .... ✓ ....

✓ .... ✓ ....

✓ .... ✓ ....

✓ .... ✓ ....

✓ .... ✓ ....

✓ .... ✓ ....

✓ .... ✓ ....

WRITE THE DETAILS OR DRAW THEM HERE.

HOW WAS YOUR TRAVEL?

○ Fun

○ Amazing

○ Fine

○ Crazy

○ Exciting

○ Boring

○ Exhausting

YOUR MOOD

YOUR RATING

RATE IT!

TRAVEL JOURNAL

When: .... Days: ....

Where: ....

Location ....

To do before leaving:

✓ .... ✓ ....

✓ .... ✓ ....

✓ .... ✓ ....

✓ .... ✓ ....

✓ .... ✓ ....

✓ .... ✓ ....

✓ .... ✓ ....

Packing Checklist:

✓ .... ✓ ....

✓ .... ✓ ....

✓ .... ✓ ....

✓ .... ✓ ....

✓ .... ✓ ....

✓ .... ✓ ....

✓ .... ✓ ....

✓ .... ✓ ....

WRITE THE DETAILS OR DRAW THEM HERE.

HOW WAS YOUR TRAVEL?

○ Fun

○ Amazing

○ Fine

○ Crazy

○ Exciting

○ Boring

○ Exhausting

YOUR MOOD

YOUR RATING

RATE IT!

TRAVEL JOURNAL

When: ....   Days: ....

Where: ....

Location ....

To do before leaving:

- ☑ ....
- ☑ ....
- ☑ ....
- ☑ ....
- ☑ ....
- ☑ ....
- ☑ ....

- ☑ ....
- ☑ ....
- ☑ ....
- ☑ ....
- ☑ ....
- ☑ ....
- ☑ ....

Packing Checklist:

- ☑ ....
- ☑ ....
- ☑ ....
- ☑ ....
- ☑ ....
- ☑ ....
- ☑ ....
- ☑ ....

- ☑ ....
- ☑ ....
- ☑ ....
- ☑ ....
- ☑ ....
- ☑ ....
- ☑ ....
- ☑ ....

WRITE THE DETAILS OR DRAW THEM HERE.

HOW WAS YOUR TRAVEL?

- ○ Fun
- ○ Amazing
- ○ Fine
- ○ Crazy
- ○ Exciting
- ○ Boring
- ○ Exhausting

YOUR MOOD

YOUR RATING

RATE IT!

TRAVEL JOURNAL

When: ....

Days: ....

Where: ....

Location ....

To do before leaving:

☑ .... ☑ ....

☑ .... ☑ ....

☑ .... ☑ ....

☑ .... ☑ ....

☑ .... ☑ ....

☑ .... ☑ ....

☑ .... ☑ ....

Packing Checklist:

☑ .... ☑ ....

☑ .... ☑ ....

☑ .... ☑ ....

☑ .... ☑ ....

☑ .... ☑ ....

☑ .... ☑ ....

☑ .... ☑ ....

☑ .... ☑ ....

WRITE THE DETAILS OR DRAW THEM HERE.

HOW WAS YOUR TRAVEL?

- ○ Fun
- ○ Amazing
- ○ Fine
- ○ Crazy
- ○ Exciting
- ○ Boring
- ○ Exhausting

YOUR MOOD

YOUR RATING

RATE IT!

NOTES (Observations, stories and encounters)

TRAVEL JOURNAL

When: .... Days: ....

Where: ....

Location ....

To do before leaving:

✓ ....   ✓ ....

✓ ....   ✓ ....

✓ ....   ✓ ....

✓ ....   ✓ ....

✓ ....   ✓ ....

✓ ....   ✓ ....

✓ ....   ✓ ....

Packing Checklist:

✓ ....   ✓ ....

✓ ....   ✓ ....

✓ ....   ✓ ....

✓ ....   ✓ ....

✓ ....   ✓ ....

✓ ....   ✓ ....

✓ ....   ✓ ....

✓ ....   ✓ ....

WRITE THE DETAILS OR DRAW THEM HERE.

HOW WAS YOUR TRAVEL?

O Fun

O Amazing

O Fine

O Crazy

O Exciting

O Boring

O Exhausting

YOUR MOOD

YOUR RATING

RATE IT!

TRAVEL JOURNAL

When: ....   Days: ....

Where: ....

Location ....

To do before leaving:

✓ ....   ✓ ....

✓ ....   ✓ ....

✓ ....   ✓ ....

✓ ....   ✓ ....

✓ ....   ✓ ....

✓ ....   ✓ ....

✓ ....   ✓ ....

Packing Checklist:

✓ ....   ✓ ....

✓ ....   ✓ ....

✓ ....   ✓ ....

✓ ....   ✓ ....

✓ ....   ✓ ....

✓ ....   ✓ ....

✓ ....   ✓ ....

✓ ....   ✓ ....

WRITE THE DETAILS OR DRAW THEM HERE.

HOW WAS YOUR TRAVEL?

- ◯ Fun
- ◯ Amazing
- ◯ Fine
- ◯ Crazy
- ◯ Exciting
- ◯ Boring
- ◯ Exhausting

YOUR MOOD

YOUR RATING

RATE IT!

☆ ☆ ☆ ☆ ☆ ☆ ☆ ☆ ☆ ☆

TRAVEL JOURNAL

When: ....   Days: ....

Where: ....

Location ....

To do before leaving:

✓ ....   ✓ ....

✓ ....   ✓ ....

✓ ....   ✓ ....

✓ ....   ✓ ....

✓ ....   ✓ ....

✓ ....   ✓ ....

✓ ....   ✓ ....

Packing Checklist:

✓ ....   ✓ ....

✓ ....   ✓ ....

✓ ....   ✓ ....

✓ ....   ✓ ....

✓ ....   ✓ ....

✓ ....   ✓ ....

✓ ....   ✓ ....

✓ ....   ✓ ....

WRITE THE DETAILS OR DRAW THEM HERE.

HOW WAS YOUR TRAVEL?

○ Fun
○ Amazing
○ Fine
○ Crazy
○ Exciting
○ Boring
○ Exhausting

YOUR MOOD

YOUR RATING

RATE IT!

People travel to faraway places to watch, in fascination, the people they ignore at home.
—Dagobert D. Runes

Not until we are lost do we begin to understand ourselves.
—Henry David Thoreau

TRAVEL JOURNAL

When: ....   Days: ....

Where: ....

Location ....

To do before leaving:

✓ ....   ✓ ....

✓ ....   ✓ ....

✓ ....   ✓ ....

✓ ....   ✓ ....

✓ ....   ✓ ....

✓ ....   ✓ ....

✓ ....   ✓ ....

Packing Checklist:

✓ ....   ✓ ....

✓ ....   ✓ ....

✓ ....   ✓ ....

✓ ....   ✓ ....

✓ ....   ✓ ....

✓ ....   ✓ ....

✓ ....   ✓ ....

WRITE THE DETAILS OR DRAW THEM HERE.

HOW WAS YOUR TRAVEL?

- ○ Fun
- ○ Amazing
- ○ Fine
- ○ Crazy
- ○ Exciting
- ○ Boring
- ○ Exhausting

YOUR MOOD

YOUR RATING

RATE IT!

NOTES (Observations, stories and encounters)

TRAVEL JOURNAL

When: ....   Days: ....

Where: ....

Location ....

To do before leaving:

✓ ....   ✓ ....

✓ ....   ✓ ....

✓ ....   ✓ ....

✓ ....   ✓ ....

✓ ....   ✓ ....

✓ ....   ✓ ....

✓ ....   ✓ ....

Packing Checklist:

✓ ....   ✓ ....

✓ ....   ✓ ....

✓ ....   ✓ ....

✓ ....   ✓ ....

✓ ....   ✓ ....

✓ ....   ✓ ....

✓ ....   ✓ ....

✓ ....   ✓ ....

WRITE THE DETAILS OR DRAW THEM HERE.

HOW WAS YOUR TRAVEL?

- ◯ Fun
- ◯ Amazing
- ◯ Fine
- ◯ Crazy
- ◯ Exciting
- ◯ Boring
- ◯ Exhausting

YOUR MOOD

YOUR RATING

☆ ☆ ☆ ☆ ☆

RATE IT!

TRAVEL JOURNAL

When: ....

Days: ....

Where: ....

Location ....

To do before leaving:

✓ ....   ✓ ....

✓ ....   ✓ ....

✓ ....   ✓ ....

✓ ....   ✓ ....

✓ ....   ✓ ....

✓ ....   ✓ ....

✓ ....   ✓ ....

Packing Checklist:

✓ ....   ✓ ....

✓ ....   ✓ ....

✓ ....   ✓ ....

✓ ....   ✓ ....

✓ ....   ✓ ....

✓ ....   ✓ ....

✓ ....   ✓ ....

✓ ....   ✓ ....

WRITE THE DETAILS OR DRAW THEM HERE.

HOW WAS YOUR TRAVEL?

○ Fun

○ Amazing

○ Fine

○ Crazy

○ Exciting

○ Boring

○ Exhausting

YOUR MOOD

YOUR RATING

RATE IT!

TRAVEL JOURNAL

When: ....

Days: ....

Where: ....

Location ....

To do before leaving:

☑ .... ☑ ....

☑ .... ☑ ....

☑ .... ☑ ....

☑ .... ☑ ....

☑ .... ☑ ....

☑ .... ☑ ....

☑ .... ☑ ....

Packing Checklist:

☑ .... ☑ ....

☑ .... ☑ ....

☑ .... ☑ ....

☑ .... ☑ ....

☑ .... ☑ ....

☑ .... ☑ ....

☑ .... ☑ ....

☑ .... ☑ ....

WRITE THE DETAILS OR DRAW THEM HERE.

HOW WAS YOUR TRAVEL?

- ◯ Fun
- ◯ Amazing
- ◯ Fine
- ◯ Crazy
- ◯ Exciting
- ◯ Boring
- ◯ Exhausting

YOUR MOOD

YOUR RATING

RATE IT!

TRAVEL JOURNAL

When: ....   Days: ....

Where: ....

Location ....

To do before leaving:

✓ ....   ✓ ....

✓ ....   ✓ ....

✓ ....   ✓ ....

✓ ....   ✓ ....

✓ ....   ✓ ....

✓ ....   ✓ ....

✓ ....   ✓ ....

Packing Checklist:

✓ ....   ✓ ....

✓ ....   ✓ ....

✓ ....   ✓ ....

✓ ....   ✓ ....

✓ ....   ✓ ....

✓ ....   ✓ ....

✓ ....   ✓ ....

✓ ....   ✓ ....

WRITE THE DETAILS OR DRAW THEM HERE.

HOW WAS YOUR TRAVEL?

- ◯ Fun
- ◯ Amazing
- ◯ Fine
- ◯ Crazy
- ◯ Exciting
- ◯ Boring
- ◯ Exhausting

YOUR MOOD

YOUR RATING

RATE IT!

TRAVEL JOURNAL

When: ....   Days: ....

Where: ....

Location ....

To do before leaving:

- ✓ ....   ✓ ....
- ✓ ....   ✓ ....
- ✓ ....   ✓ ....
- ✓ ....   ✓ ....
- ✓ ....   ✓ ....
- ✓ ....   ✓ ....
- ✓ ....   ✓ ....

Packing Checklist:

- ✓ ....   ✓ ....
- ✓ ....   ✓ ....
- ✓ ....   ✓ ....
- ✓ ....   ✓ ....
- ✓ ....   ✓ ....
- ✓ ....   ✓ ....
- ✓ ....   ✓ ....
- ✓ ....   ✓ ....

WRITE THE DETAILS OR DRAW THEM HERE.

HOW WAS YOUR TRAVEL?

- ◯ Fun
- ◯ Amazing
- ◯ Fine
- ◯ Crazy
- ◯ Exciting
- ◯ Boring
- ◯ Exhausting

YOUR MOOD

YOUR RATING

RATE IT!

NOTES (Observations, stories and encounters)

TRAVEL JOURNAL

When: ....   Days: ....

Where: ....

Location ....

To do before leaving:

✓ ....   ✓ ....

✓ ....   ✓ ....

✓ ....   ✓ ....

✓ ....   ✓ ....

✓ ....   ✓ ....

✓ ....   ✓ ....

✓ ....   ✓ ....

Packing Checklist:

✓ ....   ✓ ....

✓ ....   ✓ ....

✓ ....   ✓ ....

✓ ....   ✓ ....

✓ ....   ✓ ....

✓ ....   ✓ ....

✓ ....   ✓ ....

✓ ....   ✓ ....

WRITE THE DETAILS OR DRAW THEM HERE.

HOW WAS YOUR TRAVEL?

- ○ Fun
- ○ Amazing
- ○ Fine
- ○ Crazy
- ○ Exciting
- ○ Boring
- ○ Exhausting

YOUR MOOD

YOUR RATING

RATE IT!

TRAVEL JOURNAL

When: ....

Days: ....

Where: ....

Location ....

To do before leaving:

☑ ....
☑ ....
☑ ....
☑ ....
☑ ....
☑ ....
☑ ....

☑ ....
☑ ....
☑ ....
☑ ....
☑ ....
☑ ....
☑ ....

Packing Checklist:

☑ ....
☑ ....
☑ ....
☑ ....
☑ ....
☑ ....
☑ ....
☑ ....

☑ ....
☑ ....
☑ ....
☑ ....
☑ ....
☑ ....
☑ ....
☑ ....

WRITE THE DETAILS OR DRAW THEM HERE.

HOW WAS YOUR TRAVEL?

○ Fun

○ Amazing

○ Fine

○ Crazy

○ Exciting

○ Boring

○ Exhausting

YOUR MOOD

YOUR RATING

RATE IT!

TRAVEL JOURNAL

When: ....   Days: ....

Where: ....

Location ....

To do before leaving:

✓ ....   ✓ ....

✓ ....   ✓ ....

✓ ....   ✓ ....

✓ ....   ✓ ....

✓ ....   ✓ ....

✓ ....   ✓ ....

✓ ....   ✓ ....

Packing Checklist:

✓ ....   ✓ ....

✓ ....   ✓ ....

✓ ....   ✓ ....

✓ ....   ✓ ....

✓ ....   ✓ ....

✓ ....   ✓ ....

✓ ....   ✓ ....

✓ ....   ✓ ....

WRITE THE DETAILS OR DRAW THEM HERE.

HOW WAS YOUR TRAVEL?

- ◯ Fun
- ◯ Amazing
- ◯ Fine
- ◯ Crazy
- ◯ Exciting
- ◯ Boring
- ◯ Exhausting

YOUR MOOD

YOUR RATING

RATE IT!

☆ ☆ ☆ ☆ ☆ ☆ ☆ ☆ ☆ ☆

TRAVEL JOURNAL

When: ....

Days: ....

Where: ....

Location ....

To do before leaving:

✓ ....
✓ ....
✓ ....
✓ ....
✓ ....
✓ ....
✓ ....

✓ ....
✓ ....
✓ ....
✓ ....
✓ ....
✓ ....
✓ ....

Packing Checklist:

✓ ....
✓ ....
✓ ....
✓ ....
✓ ....
✓ ....
✓ ....
✓ ....

✓ ....
✓ ....
✓ ....
✓ ....
✓ ....
✓ ....
✓ ....
✓ ....

WRITE THE DETAILS OR DRAW THEM HERE.

HOW WAS YOUR TRAVEL?

- ◯ Fun
- ◯ Amazing
- ◯ Fine
- ◯ Crazy
- ◯ Exciting
- ◯ Boring
- ◯ Exhausting

YOUR MOOD

YOUR RATING

RATE IT!

TRAVEL JOURNAL

When: ....

Days: ....

Where: ....

Location ....

To do before leaving:

- ✓ ....
- ✓ ....
- ✓ ....
- ✓ ....
- ✓ ....
- ✓ ....
- ✓ ....

- ✓ ....
- ✓ ....
- ✓ ....
- ✓ ....
- ✓ ....
- ✓ ....
- ✓ ....

Packing Checklist:

- ✓ ....
- ✓ ....
- ✓ ....
- ✓ ....
- ✓ ....
- ✓ ....
- ✓ ....
- ✓ ....

- ✓ ....
- ✓ ....
- ✓ ....
- ✓ ....
- ✓ ....
- ✓ ....
- ✓ ....
- ✓ ....

WRITE THE DETAILS OR DRAW THEM HERE.

HOW WAS YOUR TRAVEL?

○ Fun

○ Amazing

○ Fine

○ Crazy

○ Exciting

○ Boring

○ Exhausting

YOUR MOOD

YOUR RATING

RATE IT!

TRAVEL JOURNAL

When: ....

Days: ....

Where: ....

Location ....

To do before leaving:

✓ ....

✓ ....

✓ ....

✓ ....

✓ ....

✓ ....

✓ ....

✓ ....

✓ ....

✓ ....

✓ ....

✓ ....

✓ ....

✓ ....

Packing Checklist:

✓ ....

✓ ....

✓ ....

✓ ....

✓ ....

✓ ....

✓ ....

✓ ....

✓ ....

✓ ....

✓ ....

✓ ....

✓ ....

✓ ....

WRITE THE DETAILS OR DRAW THEM HERE.

HOW WAS YOUR TRAVEL?

○ Fun

○ Amazing

○ Fine

○ Crazy

○ Exciting

○ Boring

○ Exhausting

YOUR MOOD

YOUR RATING

RATE IT!

NOTES (Observations, stories and encounters)

Like all great travellers, I have seen more than I remember, and
remember more than I have seen.
—Benjamin Disraeli

Don't tell me how educated you are,
tell me how much you travelled.
—Mohamed

TRAVEL JOURNAL

When: .... Days: ....

Where: ....

Location ....

To do before leaving:

✓ .... ✓ ....

✓ .... ✓ ....

✓ .... ✓ ....

✓ .... ✓ ....

✓ .... ✓ ....

✓ .... ✓ ....

✓ .... ✓ ....

Packing Checklist:

✓ .... ✓ ....

✓ .... ✓ ....

✓ .... ✓ ....

✓ .... ✓ ....

✓ .... ✓ ....

✓ .... ✓ ....

✓ .... ✓ ....

WRITE THE DETAILS OR DRAW THEM HERE.

HOW WAS YOUR TRAVEL?

○ Fun

○ Amazing

○ Fine

○ Crazy

○ Exciting

○ Boring

○ Exhausting

YOUR MOOD

YOUR RATING

RATE IT!

TRAVEL JOURNAL

When: ....   Days: ....

Where: ....

Location ....

To do before leaving:

✓ ....   ✓ ....

✓ ....   ✓ ....

✓ ....   ✓ ....

✓ ....   ✓ ....

✓ ....   ✓ ....

✓ ....   ✓ ....

✓ ....   ✓ ....

Packing Checklist:

✓ ....   ✓ ....

✓ ....   ✓ ....

✓ ....   ✓ ....

✓ ....   ✓ ....

✓ ....   ✓ ....

✓ ....   ✓ ....

✓ ....   ✓ ....

✓ ....   ✓ ....

WRITE THE DETAILS OR DRAW THEM HERE.

HOW WAS YOUR TRAVEL?

○ Fun

○ Amazing

○ Fine

○ Crazy

○ Exciting

○ Boring

○ Exhausting

YOUR MOOD

YOUR RATING

RATE IT!

TRAVEL JOURNAL

When: ....

Days: ....

Where: ....

Location ....

To do before leaving:

✓ ....
✓ ....
✓ ....
✓ ....
✓ ....
✓ ....
✓ ....

✓ ....
✓ ....
✓ ....
✓ ....
✓ ....
✓ ....
✓ ....

Packing Checklist:

✓ ....
✓ ....
✓ ....
✓ ....
✓ ....
✓ ....
✓ ....
✓ ....

✓ ....
✓ ....
✓ ....
✓ ....
✓ ....
✓ ....
✓ ....
✓ ....

WRITE THE DETAILS OR DRAW THEM HERE.

HOW WAS YOUR TRAVEL?

- ◯ Fun
- ◯ Amazing
- ◯ Fine
- ◯ Crazy
- ◯ Exciting
- ◯ Boring
- ◯ Exhausting

YOUR MOOD

YOUR RATING

RATE IT!

TRAVEL JOURNAL

When: .... Days: ....

Where: ....

Location ....

To do before leaving:

- [ ] ....
- [ ] ....
- [ ] ....
- [ ] ....
- [ ] ....
- [ ] ....
- [ ] ....

- [ ] ....
- [ ] ....
- [ ] ....
- [ ] ....
- [ ] ....
- [ ] ....
- [ ] ....

Packing Checklist:

- [ ] ....
- [ ] ....
- [ ] ....
- [ ] ....
- [ ] ....
- [ ] ....
- [ ] ....
- [ ] ....

- [ ] ....
- [ ] ....
- [ ] ....
- [ ] ....
- [ ] ....
- [ ] ....
- [ ] ....

WRITE THE DETAILS OR DRAW THEM HERE.

HOW WAS YOUR TRAVEL?

- ◯ Fun
- ◯ Amazing
- ◯ Fine
- ◯ Crazy
- ◯ Exciting
- ◯ Boring
- ◯ Exhausting

YOUR MOOD

YOUR RATING

RATE IT!

TRAVEL JOURNAL

When: ....   Days: ....

Where: ....

Location ....

To do before leaving:

- ☑ ....   ☑ ....
- ☑ ....   ☑ ....
- ☑ ....   ☑ ....
- ☑ ....   ☑ ....
- ☑ ....   ☑ ....
- ☑ ....   ☑ ....
- ☑ ....   ☑ ....

Packing Checklist:

- ☑ ....   ☑ ....
- ☑ ....   ☑ ....
- ☑ ....   ☑ ....
- ☑ ....   ☑ ....
- ☑ ....   ☑ ....
- ☑ ....   ☑ ....
- ☑ ....   ☑ ....
- ☑ ....   ☑ ....

WRITE THE DETAILS OR DRAW THEM HERE.

HOW WAS YOUR TRAVEL?

- ⭕ Fun
- ⭕ Amazing
- ⭕ Fine
- ⭕ Crazy
- ⭕ Exciting
- ⭕ Boring
- ⭕ Exhausting

YOUR MOOD

YOUR RATING

RATE IT!

NOTES (Observations, stories and encounters)

TRAVEL JOURNAL

When: ....

Days: ....

Where: ....

Location ....

To do before leaving:

- ✓ ....
- ✓ ....
- ✓ ....
- ✓ ....
- ✓ ....
- ✓ ....
- ✓ ....

- ✓ ....
- ✓ ....
- ✓ ....
- ✓ ....
- ✓ ....
- ✓ ....
- ✓ ....

Packing Checklist:

- ✓ ....
- ✓ ....
- ✓ ....
- ✓ ....
- ✓ ....
- ✓ ....
- ✓ ....
- ✓ ....

- ✓ ....
- ✓ ....
- ✓ ....
- ✓ ....
- ✓ ....
- ✓ ....
- ✓ ....
- ✓ ....

WRITE THE DETAILS OR DRAW THEM HERE.

HOW WAS YOUR TRAVEL?

- ○ Fun
- ○ Amazing
- ○ Fine
- ○ Crazy
- ○ Exciting
- ○ Boring
- ○ Exhausting

YOUR MOOD

YOUR RATING

RATE IT!

NOTES (Observations, stories and encounters)

TRAVEL JOURNAL

When: .... Days: ....

Where: ....

Location ....

To do before leaving:

✓ .... ✓ ....

✓ .... ✓ ....

✓ .... ✓ ....

✓ .... ✓ ....

✓ .... ✓ ....

✓ .... ✓ ....

✓ .... ✓ ....

Packing Checklist:

✓ .... ✓ ....

✓ .... ✓ ....

✓ .... ✓ ....

✓ .... ✓ ....

✓ .... ✓ ....

✓ .... ✓ ....

✓ .... ✓ ....

✓ .... ✓ ....

WRITE THE DETAILS OR DRAW THEM HERE.

HOW WAS YOUR TRAVEL?

○ Fun

○ Amazing

○ Fine

○ Crazy

○ Exciting

○ Boring

○ Exhausting

YOUR MOOD

YOUR RATING

RATE IT!

NOTES (Observations, stories and encounters)

TRAVEL JOURNAL

When: ....

Days: ....

Where: ....

Location ....

To do before leaving:

✓ ....
✓ ....
✓ ....
✓ ....
✓ ....
✓ ....
✓ ....

✓ ....
✓ ....
✓ ....
✓ ....
✓ ....
✓ ....
✓ ....

Packing Checklist:

✓ ....
✓ ....
✓ ....
✓ ....
✓ ....
✓ ....
✓ ....
✓ ....

✓ ....
✓ ....
✓ ....
✓ ....
✓ ....
✓ ....
✓ ....
✓ ....

WRITE THE DETAILS OR DRAW THEM HERE.

HOW WAS YOUR TRAVEL?

- ◯ Fun
- ◯ Amazing
- ◯ Fine
- ◯ Crazy
- ◯ Exciting
- ◯ Boring
- ◯ Exhausting

YOUR MOOD

YOUR RATING

RATE IT!

NOTES (Observations, stories and encounters)

TRAVEL JOURNAL

When: .... Days: ....

Where: ....

Location ....

To do before leaving:

- [ ] .... - [ ] ....
- [ ] .... - [ ] ....
- [ ] .... - [ ] ....
- [ ] .... - [ ] ....
- [ ] .... - [ ] ....
- [ ] .... - [ ] ....
- [ ] .... - [ ] ....

Packing Checklist:

- [ ] .... - [ ] ....
- [ ] .... - [ ] ....
- [ ] .... - [ ] ....
- [ ] .... - [ ] ....
- [ ] .... - [ ] ....
- [ ] .... - [ ] ....
- [ ] .... - [ ] ....
- [ ] .... - [ ] ....

WRITE THE DETAILS OR DRAW THEM HERE.

HOW WAS YOUR TRAVEL?

- ◯ Fun
- ◯ Amazing
- ◯ Fine
- ◯ Crazy
- ◯ Exciting
- ◯ Boring
- ◯ Exhausting

YOUR MOOD

YOUR RATING

RATE IT!

TRAVEL JOURNAL

When: ....

Days: ....

Where: ....

Location ....

To do before leaving:

- ✓ ....
- ✓ ....
- ✓ ....
- ✓ ....
- ✓ ....
- ✓ ....
- ✓ ....

- ✓ ....
- ✓ ....
- ✓ ....
- ✓ ....
- ✓ ....
- ✓ ....
- ✓ ....

Packing Checklist:

- ✓ ....
- ✓ ....
- ✓ ....
- ✓ ....
- ✓ ....
- ✓ ....
- ✓ ....
- ✓ ....

- ✓ ....
- ✓ ....
- ✓ ....
- ✓ ....
- ✓ ....
- ✓ ....
- ✓ ....
- ✓ ....

WRITE THE DETAILS OR DRAW THEM HERE.

HOW WAS YOUR TRAVEL?

○ Fun

○ Amazing

○ Fine

○ Crazy

○ Exciting

○ Boring

○ Exhausting

YOUR MOOD

YOUR RATING

RATE IT!

NOTES (Observations, stories and encounters)

TRAVEL JOURNAL

When: .... Days: ....

Where: ....

Location ....

To do before leaving:

☑ .... ☑ ....

☑ .... ☑ ....

☑ .... ☑ ....

☑ .... ☑ ....

☑ .... ☑ ....

☑ .... ☑ ....

☑ .... ☑ ....

Packing Checklist:

☑ .... ☑ ....

☑ .... ☑ ....

☑ .... ☑ ....

☑ .... ☑ ....

☑ .... ☑ ....

☑ .... ☑ ....

☑ .... ☑ ....

☑ .... ☑ ....

WRITE THE DETAILS OR DRAW THEM HERE.

HOW WAS YOUR TRAVEL?

○ Fun

○ Amazing

○ Fine

○ Crazy

○ Exciting

○ Boring

○ Exhausting

YOUR MOOD

YOUR RATING

RATE IT!

TRAVEL JOURNAL

When: ....   Days: ....

Where: ....

Location ....

To do before leaving:

✓ ....   ✓ ....

✓ ....   ✓ ....

✓ ....   ✓ ....

✓ ....   ✓ ....

✓ ....   ✓ ....

✓ ....   ✓ ....

✓ ....   ✓ ....

Packing Checklist:

✓ ....   ✓ ....

✓ ....   ✓ ....

✓ ....   ✓ ....

✓ ....   ✓ ....

✓ ....   ✓ ....

✓ ....   ✓ ....

✓ ....   ✓ ....

✓ ....   ✓ ....

WRITE THE DETAILS OR DRAW THEM HERE.

HOW WAS YOUR TRAVEL?

○ Fun

○ Amazing

○ Fine

○ Crazy

○ Exciting

○ Boring

○ Exhausting

YOUR MOOD

YOUR RATING

RATE IT!

NOTES (Observations, stories and encounters)

The journey not the arrival matters.
T.S. Eliot

The real voyage of discovery consists not in seeing new landscapes, but in having new eyes.
Marcel Proust

Made in the USA
Las Vegas, NV
10 March 2024

87007936R00111